THE GREAT CLOAK

JOHN MONTAGUE

The Great Cloak

*The Greeks also used it anciently, as
appeareth by Venus' mantle lined with
stars, though afterwards they changed
the form thereof into their cloaks
called* pallia, *as some of the Irish. . . .*

SPENSER

THE DOLMEN PRESS

OXFORD UNIVERSITY PRESS
NORTH AMERICA : WAKE FOREST UNIVERSITY PRESS

*Set in Pilgrim type and printed and published
in the Republic of Ireland at the Dolmen Press,
North Richmond Industrial Estate,
North Richmond Street, Dublin 1*

ISBN 0 85105 327 0 THE DOLMEN PRESS
ISBN 0 19 211884 6 OXFORD UNIVERSITY PRESS
ISBN 0 916390 07 1 WAKE FOREST UNIVERSITY PRESS

*First published 1978
Reprinted 1978
in association with Oxford University Press
and Wake Forest University Press*

*Oxford University Press,
Walton Street, Oxford OX2 6DP*

OXFORD   LONDON   GLASGOW   NEW YORK
TORONTO   MELBOURNE   WELLINGTON   CAPE TOWN
IBADAN   NAIROBI   DAR ES SALAAM   LUSAKA
KUALA LUMPUR   SINGAPORE   JAKARTA   HONG KONG   TOKYO
DELHI   BOMBAY   CALCUTTA   MADRAS   KARACHI

Wake Forest University Press

WINSTON-SALEM, NORTH CAROLINA 27109

CONTENTS

I

III

ANCHOR

PLOT

These poems should not only be read separately. A married man seeks comfort elsewhere, as his marriage breaks down. But he discovers that libertinism does not relieve his solitude. So the first section of the book ends with a slight affair which turns serious, the second with the despairing voices of a disintegrating marriage, the third with a new and growing relationship to which he pledges himself.

> As my Province burns
> I sing of love,
> Hoping to give that fiery
> Wheel a shove.

I

SEARCH

Deux corps se rapprochaient; il nait de la chaleur une fermentation, mais tout état de cette nature est passager. C'est une fleur dont il faut jouir avec volupté.

Stendhal

> To touch,
> without being touched;
> zero's discipline :
> hands of the surgeon.

MOUNT VENUS

> Forever the slim demon
> elevates his claret cup
> saying, there is but one life,
> fill and drink up, while
>
> over the villa'd suburbs
> his careless laughter rings
> before his snout vanishes
> among a lady's earrings.

THE HUNT

Chased beast, exultant huntress,
the same flood of hair.
I gripped you, you seized me.
In the battle, our limbs tangle forever.

But already impatient dawn breaks.

Blithe, surprised,
we refind our bodies.
So far, there is only someone else.

after André Frénaud

DO NOT DISTURB

A lift rising towards
or falling from, love.
Caressing glances, dart-
ing, possessive touches;
the porter's conspiracy,
distaste of the outraged.

That always strange moment
when the clothes peel away
(bark from an unknown tree)
with, not a blessing moon,
but a city's panelled skyline;
an early warning system

Before, disentangling,
through rain's soft swish,
the muted horns of taxis,
whirl of police or fire engine,
habitual sounds of loneliness
resume the mind again.

SNOWFIELD

The paleness of your flesh.

Long afterwards, I gaze happily
At my warm tracks radiating

Across that white expanse.

TRACKS

I

The vast bedroom
a hall of air,
our linked bodies
lying there.

II

As I turn to kiss
your long, black
hair, small breasts,
heat flares from
your fragrant skin,
your eyes widen as
deeper, more certain
and often, I enter
to search possession
of where your being
hides in flesh.

III

Behind our eyelids
a landscape opens,
a violet horizon
pilgrims labour across,
a sky of colours
that change, explode
a fantail of stars
the mental lightning
of sex illuminating
the walls of the skull;
a floating pleasure dome.

IV

I shall miss you
creaks the mirror
into which the scene
shortly disappears:
the vast bedroom
a hall of air, the
tracks of our bodies
fading there, while
giggling maids push
a trolley of fresh
linen down the corridor.

HAND

My hand rests on
the table between
us. As we lean to
kiss, it tightens.

Then your long
fingernails stroke
& stroke the skin.
It slowly opens

so you can rest
your fragile fist,
trembling, a
balanced butterfly.

GOLD LEAF

Love's pollen
lies lightly
on your skin;
a golden dust.
Let me brush
it with my wing!

CAUGHT

A slight girl and easily got rid of:
He took his pleasure in an idle dance,
Laughed to hear her cry under him,
But woke to find his body in a trance.
Wherever he walked, he seemed to see
Her approaching figure, whoever spoke
He strained for echoes of her voice,
And, in a rage of loss, turned back
To where she slept, hands clasped on
Small breasts in a posture of defence.
Conqueror turned plaintiff, he tries
To uncurl them, to see long-lashed eyes
Turn slowly up, hear a meek voice say:
'Are you back, my love, back to stay?'

GONE

I awake to dawn in a strange
place, hearing the birds acclaim
repetition with their light voices,
a defiant pattern of beauty
flagrant as the heavy blossoms
hanging wet against my window.

But ornate magnolia, Belle of Portugal
rose with its outlandish whiteness,
the grey-blue musk of eucalyptus,
seem only to stress, in a need
born of their resolute gaudiness,
one overriding fact: your absence.

CLOSED CIRCUIT

An ache, anger
thunder of a hurtling
waterfall in the ears:
in abrupt detail he sees
the room where she lays
  her pale, soft body
  under another's

  her petal mouth
  raised to absorb
  his probing kiss
and hears her small voice
  cry animal cries
in the hissing anguish
  the release of

  my sweet one
my darling, my love
until they fall apart
(Oh, the merciless creak
of jealousy's film)
  in a wet calm
like flowers after rain.

TALISMAN

After talking together
we move, as by a natural
progress, to make love.
Slant afternoon light

on the bed, the unlatched
window, scattered sheets
are part of a pattern
hastening towards memory

as you give yourself
to me with a cry of
joy, not hunger, while
I receive the gift

in ease, not raw desire
& all the superstructure
of the city outside —
twenty iron floors

of hotel dropping
to where the late sun
strikes the shield of
the lake, its chill towers —

are elements in a slowly
developing dream, a talisman
of calm, to invoke against
unease, to invoke against harm.

Ladies I have lain
      with in darkened rooms
sweet shudder of flesh
      behind shadowy blinds
long bars of light
      across tipped breasts
warm mounds of
      breathing sweetness
young flesh redolent
      of crumpled roses
the tender anxiety
      of the middle-aged
a hovering candle
      hiding blue veins
eloquent exhaustion
      watching light fade
as your drowsy partner
      drifts towards the
warm shores of sleep
      and you slowly awake
to confront again
      the alluring lie
of searching through
      another's pliant body
for something missing
      in your separate self
while profound night
      like a black swan
goes pluming past.

II

SEPARATION

Your mistake, *my* mistake.
Small heads writhing,
a basket of snakes.

THE SCREECH OWL

The night is a great sleeping city
where the wind breathes. It has come
from far to our bed's safety, this June
midnight. You sleep, a hazel tree rustles,
I am led towards the borders of dream.
Comes that cry, nearing, disappearing,
a gleam fleeing through woods, or shades
some might say, which flit through hell.
(Of this midsummer night cry, how much
I might say, and of your gaze.) Though it is
only a bird called the screech owl, calling
from the depths of these suburban woods. And
already our bodies smell of the rankness
of the small hours, as under the warm skin
the bone pierces, while stars fade at street ends.

after Phillipe Jacottet

LATE

I return late, on tiptoe.
Moonlight pours over the bed
and your still, sleeping head
reproving silently
my stealthy prowler's tread.

DARKNESS

Against my knees
you lie, curled
like an animal
seeking warmth,
affection, the
caressing hand,
& speak sadly of

dreams you must
endure, left alone
at the mercy
of the powers
of night, when
darkness holds
all the land.

CHILDLESS

Body
a garden summer ignores.

Body
a funeral where no one weeps.

Body
a husk without a kernel.

Body
a stone buried in earth.

23

TEARING

I

I sing your pain
as best I can
   seek
like a gentle man
   to assume
the proffered blame.

But the pose breaks.
The sour facts remain.
   It takes
two to make or break
   a marriage.
Unhood the falcon!

II

Pastourelle

Hands on the pommel,
long dress trailing
over polished leather
riding boots, a spur
jutting from the heel,
& beneath, the bridle path,
strewn with rusty apples,
brown knobs of chestnut,
meadow saffron and acorn.

Then we were in the high
ribbed dark of the trees
where animals move stealth-
ily, coupling & killing,

24

while we talked nostalgically
of our lives, bedevilled
& betrayed by lost love —
the furious mole, tunnelling
near us his tiny kingdom —

& how slowly we had come
to where we wished each other
happiness, far and apart, as
a hawk circled the wood,
& a victim cried, the sound
of hooves rising & falling
upon bramble & fern, while
a thin growth of rain gathered about us, like a cowl.

III

Never

In the gathering dark
I caress your head
as you thrash out
flat words of pain :
'There is no way back,
I can feel it happening;
we shall never be
what we were, again.'

Never, a solemn bell
tolling through
that darkening room
where I cradle your head,

25

only a glimmer left
in the high window
over what was once
our marriage bed.

IV

Refrain

I sit in autumn sunlight
on a hotel terrace as I did

when our marriage had begun,
our public honeymoon,

try to unsnarl what went wrong,
shouldering all the blame,

but no chivalric mode,
courtesy's silent discipline

softens the pain
when something is ending

and the tearing begins :
'We shall never be

what we were, again.'
Old love's refrain.

IN THE DARK

As the thunderstorm
hovers over the car

your hand roves
over me, a frantic claw,

your mouth clamps
upon mine.

To kiss, in hunger
to kiss, in friendliness

not this salt
smart of anger and despair

an acrid salutation
bruising the lips.

After, in the dark
a voice in anger

by the roadside
a worn car tyre

smouldering, a stench
of burning rubber.

SHE WALKS ALONE

In the white city of Evora, absence accosted me.
You were reading in bed, while I walked all night
      alone.
Were you worried about me, or drifting towards
      sleep?

I saw the temple of Diana, bone white in the moon-
      light.
I made a private prayer to her, for strength to
      continue:
Not since convent days have I prayed so earnestly.

A dog came out of the shadows, brushed against my
      leg.
He followed me everywhere, pushing his nose into
      my hand.
Soon the cats appeared, little scraggy bundles of need.

There were more monuments, vivid as hallucinations.
Suddenly, a young man stepped out of the shadows:
I was not terrified, as I might have been at home.

Besides, he was smiling & gentle as you used to be.
'A kiss' he pleads 'a kiss' in soft Portuguese.
I quickened my step, but he padded behind me.

He looked so young, my heart went out to him.
I stopped in the shadows under the Cathedral.
We kissed, and the tears poured down my face.

28

We float in sunlight, inside the blue swimming pool,
two fish in a glass bowl. And from your silence I
realise that you would wish I were someone else. And
that, at the same time as wishing me away, you are
angry with me for causing that thought. My aware-
ness of your desire, the thought of caresses which I
cannot keep from imagining in detail (two bodies
crawling over each other, enslimed with love), caresses I can no longer hope to receive, causes me more
and more pain. And above all the despair when your
eyes brighten at some mention of her, like a dreaming
child. For you have always kept something of the
eagerness of a child, looking forward to the next treat.
But I have lost both faith and hope, and live on suffer-
ance, an old tower crumbling by the water's edge.

SEPARATION

Two fish float :

one slowly downstream
into the warm
currents of the known

the other tugging
against the stream,
disconsolate twin,

the golden
marriage hook
tearing its throat.

WEDGE

Rue Daguerre, how we searched
till we found it! Beyond
the blunt pawed lion of Denfert
to where, after the bustle
of an open stalled market
you halt, before stooping
into a cobbled courtyard.

Symbol of the good life
this silence, each bend-
ing to his chosen task;
a Japanese framer, tire-
less and polite, tending
a grafted cherry tree as
if it were his exiled self

which foamed to brief
and splendid blossom
each European spring.
The florist who made a
speciality of wreaths,
flower woven cartwheels
a cortège on his walls

smothered at Christmas
by fragrant limbs of fir.
The old woman stitching
moleskin sacks and bags
while her gross, gelded
cat dozed towards death
along its sunlit bench.

On Sunday mornings,
white canes racked,
two blind men played
the accordeon, those
simple rippling tunes
that tore the heart;
sous les toits de Paris.

Or, *la vie en rose,*
setting for a shared
life, slowly broken,
wrenched, torn apart,
change driving its
blunt wedge through
what seemed permanent:

the cobbles uprooted,
the framer beheaded
in a multiple accident,
a giant tower hulking
over the old market,
the traffic's roar
(waves grinding near

a littered shore)
while time whirls
faster and faster,
*j'attendrai tous
les jours,* a blind
accordeon playing
to a funeral wreath.

L'ADIEU

I gathered this sprig of heather
The autumn is dead   remember
We shall never again see each other
Smell of time odour of heather
I wait for you   remember

after Apollinaire

33

NO MUSIC

I'll tell you a sore truth, little understood.
It's harder to leave, than to be left:
To stay, to leave, both sting wrong.

You will always have me to blame,
Can dream we might have sailed on;
From absence's rib, a warm fiction.

But I must recognise what I have done,
And if it fails, accept the burden
Of the harm done to you & another one.

To tear up old love by the roots,
To trample on past affections:
There is no music for so harsh a song.

*

A blind cripple, trailing
His stick across cobbles;
A butterfly with a torn wing.

THE WANDERER'S SONG

I stalk off through the morning fields.
The little house dwindles behind me;
If I glanced back I might not see it.

Shaking a handkerchief, she turns indoors.
For hours she will sit there, brooding,
Loathing me, yet wishing me home.

Along the cliffs I wander, hearing
The lean gulls cry. I hardly know where
I am bound, but I like the morning air.

I feel the sun warm on my shoulders.
My feet sink in earth, rough grass;
To be alone again, strange happiness!

THE BLUE ROOM

Tired, turning, restless
the insomniac feels the pulse
that feeds his body

pity for his past,
fear of the future,
his spirit beats

along his veins
a ceaseless, dervish dance
which defies oblivion.

Night a pit into
which he falls & falls
endlessly, his memories

a circle of hobbyhorses
grinding up and down
gross, grinning teeth

until dawn biting
its throat, a bird
starts its habitual

terrible, day-beginning cry.
The trees emerge from the stillness.
The raindrop bends the leaf.

SHE WRITES

i: *No News*

'Dear one, no news from you so long.
I went and came back from the Alps,
I went and came back from the Vosges.
The boy you liked, the forester's son,
Who kept a yellow fox cub in the house
Now has a tame deer, which bumps wildly
Against the furniture, on bony stilts.
More news of shooting in the North.
Did you go to Enniskillen, as you said?
Lying alone at night, I see your body
Like Art O Leary, that elegy you translated,
Lying in a ditch before me, dead.
The cherry tree is alight in the garden.
Come back to our little courtyard,' she said.

ii: *Alone*

Again your lost, hurt voice;
'I hope this never happens you,
I wouldn't wish it upon anyone:
To live and dance in lonely fire,
To lie awake at night, listening
For a step that cannot come.
Of course I gave away the cats.
I found their lovesick cries
More than I could easily bear.
Remember our favourite Siamese?
The moment you entered the yard
He and I would both lift an ear.
Now he is dead, you are gone.
I sleep in the same room, alone.'

SHE DREAMS

Habituée of darkness I have become.
Familiar of the secret feeding grounds
Where terror and dismay ceaselessly hatch,
Black forms curling and uncoiling;
The demons of the night feel like friends.

Something furry brushes along my arm,
A bat or screech owl hurtling by.
I clamber over stained rocks and find
The long gathered contents of our house
Swarming with decay, a filthied nest.

I came to where the eggs lay in the grass.
I watched them for a long time, warming them
With my swollen eyes. One after another
They chipped and scraggy heads appeared;
The embryos of our unborn children.

They turn towards me, croaking 'Mother!'
I gather them up into my apron
But the shape of the house has fallen
And you are asleep by the water's edge:
A wind and wave picked skeleton.

LAMENT

In anger against
that strictness
in myself I wish
to ease, yet keep,

Dissolve that I
might the more
eagerly love;
learn to give.

As I have learnt
on occasions to weep
like a stricken animal
knowing nothing but

What was ailing me.
But animals don't cry
you said, as I might
lightly have agreed

Had I not heard one
howl for her companion
all night long, with
a more than human

Grief, an unashamed,
unconstrained, teeth-baring
lament, one creature
in a fury of loss

Bearing witness to
the passage of another
into the untrespassable
realms of the dead.

HERBERT STREET REVISITED
for *Madeleine*

I

A light is burning late
in this Georgian Dublin street:
someone is leading our old lives!

And our black cat scampers again
through the wet grass of the convent garden
upon his masculine errands.

The pubs shut: a released bull,
Behan shoulders up the street,
topples into our basement, roaring 'John!'

A pony and donkey cropped flank
by flank under the trees opposite;
short neck up, long neck down,

as Nurse Mullen knelt by her bedside
to pray for her lost Mayo hills,
the bruised bodies of Easter Volunteers.

Animals, neighbours, treading the pattern
of one time and place into history,
like our early marriage, while

tall windows looked down upon us
from walls flushed light pink or salmon
watching and enduring succession.

II

As I leave, you whisper,
'don't betray our truth'
and like a ghost dancer,
invoking a lost tribal strength
I halt in tree-fed darkness

to summon back our past,
and celebrate a love that eased
so kindly, the dying bone,
enabling the spirit to sing
of old happiness, when alone.

III

So put the leaves back on the tree,
put the tree back in the ground,
let Brendan trundle his corpse down
the street singing, like Molly Malone.

Let the black cat, tiny emissary
of our happiness, streak again
through the darkness, to fall soft
clawed into a landlord's dustbin.

Let Nurse Mullen take the last
train to Westport, and die upright
in her chair, facing a window
warm with the blue slopes of Nephin.

And let the pony and donkey come —
look, someone has left the gate open —
like hobbyhorses linked in
the slow motion of a dream

parading side by side, down
the length of Herbert Street,
rising and falling, lifting
their hooves through the moonlight.

III

ANCHOR

Is maith an t-ancoir an t-iarta:
the hearth is a good anchor.

Old Irish Proverb

A MEETING

The son of the King of the Moy
met a girl in green woods on mid-summer's day :
she gave him black fruit from thorns
& the full of his arms
of strawberries, where they lay.

from the ninth-century Irish

Silence
& damp night air
Flowing from the garden.

Like a young girl
Dissatisfied with
Her mythic burden
Ceres, corn goddess,
Mistress of summer,
Steps sure-footed over
The sweet smelling
Bundles of grass.
Her abundant body is
Compounded of honey
& gold, the spike
Of each small nipple
A wild strawberry —
Fulfilled in
Spite of herself
She exchanges with
The moon the pale
Gold disc of her face.

BACK

The friendly moon
that overlooks
our twinned destinies
appeared last night
in the cold bright
winter sky;
I knew you had
come back.

ALLEGIANCE

Beyond the village
herds browse peacefully
behind a barred wooden gate,
a warm Constable scene
of swirling shadows & silence;
a river's murmuring presence.

In their cumbrous circle
the huge stones stand,
completing the plain,
attending the dawn,
dew on granite, damp
on a sword blade.

Slowly, in moonlight
I drop to one knee,
solemn as a knight
obeying an ancient precept,
natural as cattle
stooping in river mist.

Walking late
we share night sounds
so delicate the heart misses
a beat to hear them :

shapes in the half-dark
where the deer feed or
rest, the radar of small
ears & horns still alert
under the glooming boles
of the great oaks
                                    to unfold
their knees from the wet grass
with a single thrust & leap away
stiff-legged, in short, jagged
bursts as we approach
                                    stars lining
our path through the woods
with a low coiling mist
over the nocturnal meadows
so that we seem to wade
through the filaments
of a giant silver web
the brain crevices of a cloud.

                    *

Bleached and white
as a fish's belly,
a road curves towards the city
which, with the paling dawn,

47

will surge towards activity again,
the bubble of the Four Courts
overruling the stagnant quays,
their ghostly Viking prows,

and the echoing archways,
tenebrous walls of the Liberties
where we briefly share a life
to which we must return

as we circle uncertainly
towards a home, your
small, damp hand in mine,
no heavier than a leaf.

SIGNS

I have grown accustomed to signs & marvels,
A tree that leaned & spoke, a timely moon,
A star wandering where no star had been,
A six pointed star, the sign of union.
We share intuitions like a religion.

SONG

Let me share with you
a glimpse of richness:
two swans startled me
turning low over the Lee,
looking for a nestling place.
I thought of us, our need
for a place to lay our heads;
our flight secret, unheralded.

By the curl and gleam
of water, my sadness
was washed away:
the air was bright
and clear as your forehead,
the linked swans
reached the wood:
my love, come here to stay.

WORKING DREAM

At the end of a manuscript
I was studying, a secret message.
A star, a honeycomb, a seashell,
The stately glory of a peacock's tail
Spiralled colour across the page
To end with a space between a lean I
And a warm and open-armed You.

An hour later, you were at the door;
I learnt the world that space was for.

BLESSING

A feel of warmth in this place.
In winter air, a scent of harvest.
No form of prayer is needed,
When by sudden grace attended.
Naturally, we fall from grace.
Mere humans, we forget what light
Led us, lonely, to this place.

She sings a little
Off-key, for her
Coaxing lover
Who soothes her
To remember when
A huge figure —
The shadow of
Her father, fell
Across her crib,
Harshly shouting,
Startling the rattle
In her throat, and
When the bough
Breaks, she falls
Again, to feel
A different arm
Holding her up,
Safe and sound,
Above the void,
On the tree-top.

AFTER A QUARREL

Like a team of horses,
manes lightstreaming,
we race together,
close, and separate.
Another night of sighs
yet our love revives,
a flower in the morning

as timid, uncertain,
you bring me small
conciliatory presents,
which you hold up
in your hands, face
pursed, like a squirrel,
waiting for me to smile.

Honeycomb of reconciliation:
thigh melting into thigh,
mouth into mouth, breast
turning against ribcage:
we make love as though
this small house were
a paradigm of the universe.

SUNSET

In Loch Lene
a queen went swimming;
a redgold salmon
flowed into her
at full of evening.

from the *Félire Oengus*

WAITING

Another day of dancing summer,
Evelyn kneels on a rock, breasts
Swollen by approaching motherhood,
Hair bleached by the sea winds
To a pale as honey gold, some
Generous natural image of the good.
Sails butterfly to her nakedness,
Surprised to spy through the haze
A curved figure, sleek as a mermaid,
Or bowsprit Venus, of smooth wood,
Courting the sun and not the shade,
Seagulls aureoling her bowed head,
Translucent as Wicklow river gold;
Source of my present guilt and pride.

GOSSIP

Avoid too much notice;
learn from the hare,
crouch low, and quiet,
until the hunt passes.

PROTEST

Awed, I bent in my gauze mask
to stroke your trembling hands
while our daughter was hauled
and forced into this breathing world.
The doctor stowed the forceps, red
as for a death, blood kin of birth,
and so I relived a simple truth;
we are born, as we die, reluctantly.
Your cries had stilled, anaesthetized,
and now only her protest was heard,
a raw fleshed morsel, briefly held
aloft, or mouthing furiously behind
her transparent plastic shield,
small paws kneading, kitten blind.

LUNULA

In a warm sky
a young moon,
frail, luminous;
our first child.

THE GREAT CLOAK

for Evelyn

Smooth and long to swathe
a handsome woman's body,
a shape tall as a bell,
obedient to a fingernail.

Or to encompass her lover
as well, snug as flea deep
in featherbed, while their bodies
converse, on a green slope.

Or when the baby is born
to wrap the morsel tenderly
while beasts browse around them
naturally as in Bethlehem.

CONTENT

The slowed pulse
beat of happiness.
After you always
a trail of dogs, cats,
animals and children
waiting to be petted
and fed; the wholesome
litter of love.

CHILD

for Una

A firefly gleams, then
fades upon your cheek.
Now you hide beneath
everything I write;
love's invisible ink,
heart's watermark.

THE POINT

Rocks jagged in morning mist.
At intervals, the foghorn sounds
From the white lighthouse rock
Lonely as cow mourning her calf,
Groaning, belly deep, desperate.

I assisted at such failure once;
A night-long fight to save a calf
Born finally, with broken neck.
It flailed briefly on the straw,
A wide-eyed mother straddling it.

Listen carefully. This is different.
It sounds to guide, not lament.
When the defining light is powerless,
Ships hesitating down the strait
Hear its harsh voice as friendliness.

Upstairs my wife & daughter sleep.
Our two lives have separated now
But I would send my voice to yours
Cutting through the shrouding mist
Like some friendly signal in distress.

The fog is lifting, slowly.
Flag high, a new ship is entering.
The opposite shore unveils itself,
Bright in detail as a painting,
Alone, but equal to the morning.

EDGE

Edenlike as your name
this sea's edge garden
where we rest, beneath
the clarity of a lighthouse.

To fly into risk,
attempt the dream,
cast off, as we have done,
requires true luck

who know ourselves
blessed to have found
between this harbour's arms
a sheltering home

where the vast
tides of the Atlantic
lift to caress
rose coloured rocks.

So fate relents.
Hushed and calm,
safe and secret,
on the edge is best.

ACKNOWLEDGEMENTS

The third section of this book first appeared in the Canadian magazine, *Exile* (Toronto) as did the Frenaud translation. Acknowledgements are also due to *Back Door*, *B.B.C.*, *Cyphers*, *France-Ireland* (Lille), *Gorey Detail*, *Hibernia*, *The Humanist*, *Icarus*, *The Irish Press*, *The Irish Times*, *The Listener*, *The Literary Review*, *Modern Poetry in Translation*, *New Statesman*, *Outposts*, *Poems 1976–77*, *Stand*, *The Scotsman*.